The Cockermouth Flo[od]

19-20 November 2009

Cockermouth Mountain Rescue Team

Two swollen rivers, The Derwent and the Cocker, merge below the Brewery Bridge. The time is 2.30 pm on Thursday 19 November and the levels are still rising.

Sandbags are placed on the wall near the Brewery Bridge to try and keep the water out but the level continued to rise, eventually covering the platform of the bridge and completely destroying the railings.

Cockermouth Mountain Rescue Team

Tracey Atkinson

The footbridge leading over the river Cocker to Jennings brewery at 2.30 pm on Thursday 19 November. Later that evening the bridge was covered. **Inset:** The aftermath. The right side of the railings are completely bent over flat and the left hand railings are in the water.

Aidan Lucey

Sandbagging Sullart Street in the early evening of Thursday 19 November as the flood, in the background, comes ever nearer.

Cockermouth Mountain Rescue Team

Waterloo Street: evacuating residents less than one hour before the floods arrive. The Police had alerted the Cockermouth team early about the likely flooding. Fortunately the evacuation was able to start before the flood waters engulfed Waterloo Street, shortly after this picture was taken.

Looking west on Main Street at 1.00 pm Thursday. The lorry was distributing sandbags in a vain attempt to keep the rising water out of the buildings.

Aidan Lucey

As darkness falls on Thursday evening the flood advances up Main Street to finally lap at the steps of Wordsworth House. Unfortunately worse was to come. The Police are stood in Sullart Street.

Aidan Lucey

At 6.00pm the level is steadily rising in Main Street and gradually creeping up Lowther Went.

Cockermouth Mountain Rescue Team

Looking towards Main Street and Station Street from High Sand Lane at 3.00 pm on Thursday.
Note the sandbags against the doorway to the right. Unfortunately the river was going to rise much higher during the hours of darkness.

Cockermouth Mountain Rescue Team

Looking west down Main Street at 15.30 pm on Thursday as the water steadily increases in depth. In spite of the fast current the Christmas tree is still standing.

Cockermouth Mountain Rescue Team

Cockermouth Mountain Rescue Team

Looking east down Main Street at 4.20 pm on Thursday as police and mountain rescue team members check the area. Main Street has now become a fast flowing river, getting deeper and stronger by the minute. See the inset of the red car in the middle distance.

Cockermouth Mountain Rescue Team

Rescue boat at the bottom of Station Street on Thursday night.

Boat rescue in Challoner Street. Because of the dangerously strong current along Main Street. Many rescuers were needed to control the boat as the rescue proceeded. There are three ropes attached to the boat in order that a safe rescue can be carried out.

Cockermouth Mountain Rescue Team

The current is very strong and the rescuers have to fight it to keep on their feet. Notice the height of the bow wave against the person in the reflective jacket. This rescue was carried out late on Thursday afternoon.

Cockermouth Mountain Rescue Team

The scene at 6.00 pm on Thursday at the corner of Station Road and Main Street. Darkness has fallen and the flood is still rising. Many people need rescuing from homes nearer the river. Police and volunteers worked throughout the night.

Cockermouth Mountain Rescue Team

A member of the Cockermouth team demonstrates the survival equipment necessary to keep safe in cold, wet and dangerous conditons. He is wearing a dry suit, buoyancy aid and has a Team Radio and battery in his front pocket, with a lead going a helmet camera.

Tracey Atkinson

The scene in Challoner Street at 11.30 am on the Friday morning. The level has now dropped but the extreme force exerted by the water during the night is very well illustrated by the distortion of the garage door and sections of road surface ripped from further up the street.

Cockermouth Mountain Rescue Team

Cockermouth Mountain Rescue team members check properties at the eastern end of Main Street on Friday 20 November. The time is 12.30 pm and the river is still flowing quite strongly down Main Street.

Tracey Atkinson

Dawn on Friday reveals that the flats and houses adjacent to Croft Terrace are badly flooded by the River Cocker. The helicopter in the background is probably hovering over Main Street.

Tracey Atkinson

Looking across the River Cocker to Croft Terrace flats in the left foreground.
Further back is the flooded bowling green which has now become a swimming pool.

This picture taken from the Lorton Road bridge, at 8.00 am on Friday, shows Rubby Banks completely overwhelmed by the river.

Cocker Lane Bridge at midday on Friday is still withstanding the current. The water level has now dropped and large amounts of debris have been caught up on and around the footway.

Here at Cocker Lane Bridge the river Cocker has overflowed into Rubby Banks Road during the night. The time is midday on Friday and the level has now dropped below the top of the flood barrier on the bridge.

Aidan Lucey

Cocker Lane Bridge showing the large amount of debris collected during the flood.

Cockermouth Mountain Rescue Team

Rescue from Waterloo Street at 2.00 pm on Friday. The narrow inflatable proved invaluable getting through the narrow streets and alleys. A flooded Kings Arms Lane can be seen on the left.

Cockermouth Mountain Rescue Team

This evacuation by boat is into Kings Arms Lane.

Cockermouth Mountain Rescue Team

The RAF to the rescue over Waterloo Street on Friday afternoon. The only way for some to be evacuated was from the rooftops and the mountain rescue team also went up there to help. See the next page.

Cockermouth Mountain Rescue Team members on the roofs of houses in Waterloo Street to assist with helicopter evacuation. The team members on the right are warming their hands on the heating vent above Boots pharmacy.

Cockermouth Mountain Rescue Team

A Rescue Team member wades through the floating debris at the rear of Boots Pharmacy.
It is 2.00 pm on Friday and the water is still waist deep.

Main Street in the early afternoon of Friday 20 November. The debris, including wheelie bins, cars, beer barrels all proved a hazard to rescuers. Another unexpected hazard was the wool from the shop 'upstream' on Main Street which wound itself around the street (see the car above) tangling a boat propellor and wrapping round the legs and feet of rescuers.

Cockermouth Mountain Rescue Team

Dr Peter Winterbottom and James Moore of Cockermouth Mountain Rescue Team decontaminating Swift Water Rescue Equipment back at Headquarters.

Cockermouth Mountain Rescue Team

No rescue and recovery operation can proceed efficiently without co-operation. This was the scene outside Cockermouth Mountain Rescue HQ on Saturday 21 November where a multi-agency briefing on the current situation was held.

Cockermouth Mountain Rescue Team

After the flood John Bullman of Cockermouth Mountain Rescue Team inspects the damage to Cockermouth Youth Hostel which was severely affected and is still closed at the time of writing.

Tracey Atkinson

Looking along the side of the old Town Hall. The two cars are parked on Riverside car park, the buildings over to the right are on Rubby Banks Lane, on the same side as Croft Terrace, just further along.

Members of Cockermouth and Wasdale Teams checking a van in the river to the west of Cockermouth.

John Bullman of Cockermouth Team. The team checked river water levels over the next few days as nearly all of the Environmental Agency flood level monitoring stations had been washed away.

Cockermouth Mountain Rescue Team

This photograph taken in South Street on Sunday 22 November illustrates the strength of the river flowing through the streets. Garden walls, windows and street furniture were demolished by the sheer weight, volume of water and floating debris.

MOTTRAM Natural Hair Dressing Ltd 01900 824217

Tourist Information

QUALITY ART & CRAFT MALL

Tracey Atkinson

These geese had found that swimming down Cockermouth Main Street was quite a new experience and they were there for quite a while. Eventually they were rescued and taken to a more suitable location. Jasper the Labrador was very curious about these intruders, see inset.

Cockermouth Mountain Rescue Team

The recovery begins. Before Cocker bridge can be checked for safety the debris must be removed. Here Rescue Team members provide the safety cover whilst Fire & Rescue Service remove three large trees weighing up to 4 tons from the bridge on Monday 23 November.

40

Cockermouth Mountain Rescue Team

It is difficult to believe that this massive tree was torn from its roots by the flood and carried down the river. Who knows what damage it might have done to other bridges before it reached the Cocker Bridge? All bridges must be checked for safety before they are re-opened.

Cockermouth Mountain Rescue Team

Lorton Bridge was completely destroyed. The blue pipes are carrying an emergency water supply to the houses on the other side. The car on the brink had broken down on the bridge as the flood waters rose.

Notice the cracking tarmac around and below the wheel. Luckily it survived the bridge collapse.

42

David Ramshaw

Lorton Bridge is several miles upstream from Cockermouth at Low Lorton. This photograph taken two weeks after the collapse shows the damage done. The plastic pigs on the far side of the bridge are obviously considering their predicament.

Cockermouth Mountain Rescue Team

There was a great community spirit after the flood. People were determined not to let it get them down. Here Cockermouth Rescue team put up a temporary Christmas tree, donated by Whinlatter Forest for the town. By Sunday evening the lights were switched on.

Left: the switching on ceremony.   **Right:** the Cockermouth Mechanics Brass Band plays at the Rescue team headquarters.

Cockermouth Mountain Rescue Team

The devastation caused by the flooding attracted intense media interest. Station Street on the Monday after the floods was still full of television, radio and press vans, as local people were interviewed about their terrible experiences during the previous four days.

David Ramshaw

David Ramshaw

Flooded out businesses were badly affected by the floods but, within a few days, many were getting started again in temporary accommodation. Here The New Bookshop, is now sharing accommodation with several other businesses in Mitchell's Auction Company premises.

WELCOME TO SANDAIR

GOCKERMOUTH CRICKET GLUB

NEXT HOME MATCH

SPONSORED BY

JENNINGS BEERS

Cockermouth Mountain Rescue Team

Cockermouth Cricket Club suffered greatly in the flood. The Clubhouse was flooded and the pitch left covered in debris .